Crown and the Shield

D.S.Pais

Ukiyoto Publishing

All global publishing rights are held by
Ukiyoto Publishing

Published in 2024

Content Copyright © D.S.Pais

ISBN 9789362694584

All rights reserved.
No part of this publication may be reproduced, transmitted, or stored in a retrieval system, in any form by any means, electronic, mechanical, photocopying, recording or otherwise, without the prior permission of the publisher.

The moral rights of the author have been asserted.

This is a work of fiction. Names, characters, businesses, places, events, locales, and incidents are either the products of the author's imagination or used in a fictitious manner. Any resemblance to actual persons, living or dead, or actual events is purely coincidental.

This book is sold subject to the condition that it shall not by way of trade or otherwise, be lent, resold, hired out or otherwise circulated, without the publisher's prior consent, in any form of binding or cover other than that in which it is published.

www.ukiyoto.com

To my loving husband Brayan Cutinha, and my kids, Gavin and Glen, who have been my constant source of support and inspiration throughout this journey.

Acknowledgments

I would like to express my heartfelt thanks to my readers, family, and friends for their invaluable feedback, which has helped shape this story into its final form. My deepest appreciation also goes to my closest family members for their constructive criticism and encouragement during the writing process. Additionally, I am grateful to Zuri and the Ukiyoto team, for their tireless efforts in bringing this book to fruition.

I am indebted to my family for their patience and understanding, especially during those long hours spent at my desk. To my friends, who cheered me on every step of the way, your support means the world to me.

Finally, to the readers who embark on this journey with me, thank you for giving life to these characters and their stories. Your enthusiasm fuels my passion for storytelling, and I am endlessly grateful for the opportunity to share this adventure with you."

Contents

Chapter One	1
Chapter Two	7
Chapter Three	12
Chapter Four	16
Chapter Five	20
Chapter Six	24
Chapter Seven	29
Chapter Eight	33
Chapter Nine	38
Chapter Ten	43
Chapter Eleven	49
Chapter Twelve	54
Chapter Thirteen	58
Chapter Fourteen	62
Chapter Fifteen	66
Chapter Sixteen	71
Chapter Seventeen	76
Chapter Eighteen	79
Chapter Nineteen	83
About the Author	*85*

Chapter One

Born in the year 1442 to the esteemed union of Sir Richard Woodville and Jaqueline of Luxembourg, duchess dowager of Bedford, young Woodville was destined for greatness from the moment he drew his first breath.

At the tender age of seventeen, in the tumultuous year of 1459, Woodville's journey into the corridors of power began. Accompanying his father, Lord Rivers, to the bustling port of Sandwich, he found himself thrust into the heart of political intrigue. Tasked with equipping a formidable squadron, their aim was nothing short of challenging the authority of Richard Nevil, Earl of Warwick, over the coveted government of Calais. However, fate had other plans in store.

In a twist of fortune as cruel as it was unexpected, Lord Rivers and his entire fleet fell victim to the cunning stratagem of Warwick. Entrapped within the confines of Calais, father and son were ensnared as prisoners of the very cause they had fervently championed—the cause of Lancaster, in opposition to the burgeoning might of York.

With the ascension of King Edward IV to the throne, a seismic shift in fortune altered the trajectory of Woodville's fate. The King's marriage to Lady Elizabeth Gray, daughter of Lord Rivers and sister to

Woodville Anthony, heralded a new era of prosperity for the Woodville clan. Their erstwhile allegiance to the Lancastrian cause faded into obscurity as they basked in the glow of royal favor.

Woodville Anthony's prowess as both a warrior and a statesman soon became the stuff of legend within the hallowed halls of Edward's court. When the Lancastrians dared to raise their standard in the wilds of Northumberland, he rode alongside the King into the very heart of rebellion. At the siege of Alnwick Castle, his valor and strategic acumen earned him the admiration of his peers and the accolades of his sovereign.

In recognition of his unwavering loyalty and his sterling service to the crown, Woodville Anthony was bestowed with the highest of honors—an induction into the illustrious Order of the Garter. Yet, his trials were far from over. In the tenth year of Edward's reign, he found himself embroiled in a harrowing skirmish near Southampton, pitting his mettle against the formidable Dukes of Clarence and Warwick. Through sheer determination and tactical brilliance, he thwarted their ambitions and safeguarded the kingdom's interests.

His martial exploits notwithstanding, Woodville Anthony's diplomatic prowess was equally renowned. From negotiating delicate alliances with foreign powers to brokering treaties of peace and amity, he proved himself a master of statecraft. As Edward's trusted envoy, he traversed the length and breadth of Europe, weaving webs of diplomacy that bound nations together in common cause.

In a spectacle as grand as it was perilous, he found himself locked in mortal combat with none other than Anthony Count de la Roche, the notorious bastard of Burgundy. In the hallowed grounds of Smithfield, amidst a throng of cheering spectators, the two titans clashed in a duel.

The year was spectacular —it was the year of Lady Margaret's nuptials to Charles the Hardy, last Duke of Burgundy. And in this grand pageant of love and honor, Wydeville Anthony emerged triumphant, his sword arm raised in victory as the crowd roared their acclaim. For in that fleeting moment, he embodied the very spirit of chivalry—the indomitable courage, the unwavering resolve, the steadfast loyalty—that defined the age in which he lived.

A few years ago, Richard, Duke of York, the father of Edward IV, was a figure of both reverence and fear—a man whose ambitions knew no bounds.

It began not with the clash of armies or the thunder of cannons, but with the quiet murmurs of the parliament—a gathering of nobles and statesmen convened to decide the fate of a kingdom. There, Richard, Duke of York, laid claim to the crown, his voice resounding with the echo of generations past. Whether for right or favor, his cause was advanced, and King Henry, despite his royal blood, found himself cast aside in favor of the Duke's rightful claim.

But the Duke, impatient and ambitious, could not abide the slow march of time. Intent on seizing power before his appointed hour, he sought to sow discord and dissent within the realm, plotting to usurp the throne even as King Henry still drew breath. Yet, his designs were thwarted, and at Wakefield, amidst the chaos of battle, the Duke met his end, his dreams of kingship shattered upon the cold steel of his enemies' blades.

Left behind were his three sons—Edward, George, and Richard—a triumvirate of ambition and pride, each vying for supremacy in a world rife with treachery and intrigue. Edward, the eldest and most determined, avenged his father's death and claimed the crown for his own, while George, Duke of Clarence, found himself ensnared in a web of jealousy.

In the year 1461, as the dust settled upon the battlefield where the fate of England had been decided, King Edward IV stood victorious, his crown secured upon his brow. Amidst the triumph and glory, a shadow lingered—a shadow born of a promise made in the heat of battle, a promise that would bind him to a woman.

Lady Eleanor Talbot stood beside her king, her heart aflutter with anticipation as the solemn words of matrimony fell upon her ears. And there, amidst the flickering candlelight and the fragrant incense, a priest—Robert Stillington, the Bishop of Bath and Wells—bore witness to their union.

But fate, that fickle mistress, had other plans in store. For Lady Eleanor, though bound by the ties of marriage, was still very much alive when King Edward's eyes wandered to another—a woman whose beauty and grace would ignite a passion that would consume his soul.

Enter Elizabeth Woodville—a widow of noble birth, her heart heavy with the weight of loss and longing. As she knelt before the king, petitioning for the restoration of her modest lands, little did she know that her life was about to take a dramatic turn—a turn that would see her rise from the ashes of grief to claim her rightful place by his side.

King Edward, captivated by her ethereal beauty and beguiling charm, found himself ensnared in the tendrils of her allure. Though she rebuffed his advances with virtuous resolve, her presence lingered in his thoughts, her image haunting his dreams. And so, spurred on by a love that defied reason and convention, he resolved to make her his queen.

But such a union was not without its detractors. For King Edward's mother, the formidable Duchess of York, viewed his alliance with disdain, deeming it unworthy of his royal station. With a steely resolve born of maternal concern, she counseled him against the folly of marrying a mere subject—a decision that would have far-reaching consequences for the realm.

Meanwhile, across the seas, Earl of Warwick—once the king's staunchest ally—embarked on a diplomatic mission of utmost importance. Tasked with negotiating a marriage alliance with the daughter of the King of Spain, he journeyed to foreign shores, his mind aflame with visions of glory and grandeur.Even as the Earl labored to secure the king's future, the seeds of discord were sown within the very heart of England's court.

Elizabeth, now ensconced within the king's inner circle, wielded a power and influence that belied her humble origins—a fact that did not go unnoticed by those who sought to curry favor with the crown.

As King Edward's affections turned ever more ardently towards Elizabeth, the bonds of loyalty and allegiance that once bound him to his closest confidant began to fray.

Chapter Two

In the hushed corridors of Ludlow Castle, nestled amidst the rugged beauty of the Welsh Marches, a young prince came of age. Edward, newly anointed as Prince of Wales in the heady days of June 1471, found himself thrust into a world of intrigue and ambition—a world where power was the currency of kings and princes alike.

As the sun set over Ludlow's ancient walls, casting long shadows across the land, Prince Richard, his younger brother, awaited his own moment in the spotlight. For, in the royal lineage, it had become tradition for the second son of the English sovereign to bear the title of Duke of York—a mantle of honor.

In the year 1475, John Mowbray, Duke of Norfolk, passed away. With his passing, a young girl named Anne emerged as the sole heiress to the vast Mowbray estates—a fortune that would soon become the subject of fierce contention and intrigue.

Anne de Mowbray, a mere child of five summers, found herself thrust into the center of a swirling maelstrom of ambition and greed. As the 8th Countess of Norfolk, she held the key to untold riches and influence—a prize coveted by many, yet attainable by few.

It was in this tumultuous atmosphere that Prince Richard, barely four years of age, found himself betrothed to the young heiress—a marriage arranged not out of love, but out of political expediency. For Edward IV, ever the shrewd tactician, saw in Anne de Mowbray an opportunity to further enrich his family's coffers and consolidate his grip on power.

However, scarcely three years into their betrothal, tragedy struck. Anne de Mowbray, the young bride-to-be, slipped from the mortal coil, leaving behind a grieving family and a shattered alliance.

With her passing, the Mowbray titles and estates stood poised on the brink of uncertainty. In the absence of a direct heir, the lords Howard and Berkeley, sons of sisters of the late Duke of Norfolk, emerged as the rightful claimants to the Mowbray legacy—a legacy that had once been destined for the youthful Prince Richard.It was a bitter pill to swallow for Edward IV and his ambitious brood, yet they bowed to the dictates of fate and accepted the inevitable.

Meanwhile, amidst the machinations of power, Bishop Stillington—a figure of both intrigue and fear—loomed large in the minds of the Woodvilles. If rumors of the King's first marriage were to surface, the consequences could be dire indeed.And so, in the dark recesses of the court, whispers turned to action as the Duke of Clarence, erstwhile brother to the king, found himself ensnared in a web of suspicion and deceit for having spoken about what needed to be kept in absolute secrecy. Arrested on charges both real and imagined, he became a pawn in a deadly game of power and privilege—a game where the stakes were nothing less than life itself.

But even as the Duke of Clarence languished in his cell, and then died, the truth remained elusive—a tantalizing specter that danced on the edge of perception, just out of reach. For in the murky depths of courtly intrigue, secrets lay buried like bones in the earth, waiting to be unearthed by those brave or foolish enough to seek them out.

In the year 1479, the halls of English nobility reverberated with the solemn pronouncement of a title. Edward IV, in a gesture of paternal pride and royal favor, conferred upon his first born, the earldom of Pembroke—a mark of distinction that heralded his ascent to greatness, even before his tender years had fully blossomed.

When Prince Edward, the King's heir, was but a stripling of a lad, Woodville Anthony assumed the mantle of his governance. Tasked with nurturing the princely scion's talents and tempering his character, he discharged his duties with a blend of firmness and paternal affection that endeared him to both father and son alike.

Titles alone could not forge the path of destiny, nor could they guarantee the wisdom and virtue that would one day adorn the brow of a king. And so it was that Prince Edward, heir to the throne of England, found himself placed under the watchful eye of his uncle by marriage, Anthony Woodville, second Earl Rivers—a man renowned for his scholarly pursuits and keen intellect.

In the chambers of Ludlow Castle, where the air was thick with the scent of parchment and the gentle rustle of quill upon parchment, the prince embarked upon a journey of learning and enlightenment.

In a letter penned by his father, King Edward IV, precise instructions were laid down for the upbringing and education of the young prince. Rising each morning at a convenient hour, according to his age, Prince Edward would begin his day with the solemn rites of matins and Mass—a sacred ritual that would set the tone for the hours that followed.

After a hearty breakfast, the prince's education would commence in earnest, guided by the principles of "virtuous learning" and the teachings of noble scholars. His mind would be nourished with tales of valor and virtue, of honor and cunning, instilling within him the seeds of greatness and the virtues befitting a future monarch.

Even as the prince delved into the realms of literature and learning, his father's keen eye remained ever watchful, guarding against the snares of vice and immorality. No habitual swearer or brawler, no backbiter or common hazarder, would be allowed to poison the prince's mind or corrupt his soul. For King Edward IV, mindful of his own failings, was determined to spare his son the pitfalls of temptation and moral decay.

And so, under the tutelage of Earl Rivers and his esteemed retinue of tutors and mentors, Prince Edward blossomed into a paragon of scholarly virtue. His knowledge of literature was unparalleled, his discourse elegant, his understanding profound. Whether in verse or prose, he could declaim with the eloquence of a seasoned orator, captivating all who were fortunate enough to hear his words.

It was not only his intellect that endeared him to his subjects; it was his demeanor, his bearing, his very presence. With a dignity that belied his tender years and a charm that could melt the stoniest of hearts, he moved through the world with the grace and poise of a true prince. And so, as the curtains were drawn and the day gave way to night, Prince Edward would retire to his chambers, his mind alive with the wonders of the world and the promise of tomorrow. In the night, the Prince drifted into the realm of dreams, watched over by his devoted attendants.

Chapter Three

There existed a faction of wise men, whose discerning eyes penetrated the veils of pretense, alleging that Richard's outward resistance to the demise of his brother George the Duke of Clarence concealed a more insidious truth. While he feigned opposition to the Duke of Clarence's untimely demise, it was whispered that Richard harbored secret desires for the throne, envisioning himself as the rightful successor to King Edward.

Richard, ever calculating and ambitious, had long plotted his ascent to power during King Edward's reign, envisioning himself as the rightful heir in the event of his brother's demise. The death of George, therefore, was viewed as a fortuitous event by those who suspected Richard's Machiavellian machinations. For with George out of the picture, Richard's path to the throne seemed unimpeded, whether by assuming guardianship over his young nephews or by seizing power for himself.

Henry's death, was attributed to "pure displeasure and melancholy," a convenient explanation that absolved King Edward IV of any culpability. Upon learning of the death of his son and the capture of his wife, Henry succumbed to despair, his spirit broken by the complete annihilation of his family. Such was the narrative propagated by Edward's court, painting

Henry's demise as a tragic consequence of his own despair rather than as a calculated act of political expediency.

The dagger purported to have ended Henry's life, enshrined among the relics of Reading Abbey, bore silent witness to the secrets that lay buried beneath layers of deception. The victors inscribe their tales upon the scrolls of memory, while the voices of the vanquished are silenced by the passage of time.

And so it was, on a fateful night shrouded in darkness, that King Henry met his end within the confines of the Tower of London. The 21st day of May bore witness to the culmination of Richard's ambition, as he stood amidst a retinue of loyalists, poised to enact the final act in his Machiavellian drama. With the stroke of a dagger, Henry's fate was sealed, his life extinguished to serve the interests of Edward's burgeoning reign.

In the cold light of dawn, Henry's lifeless form was borne through the streets of London. Glaives and staves formed a somber procession around his bier, eclipsing the feeble glow of torches that sought to illuminate the path to his final resting place. Within the hallowed halls of St. Paul's Cathedral, Henry's corpse lay in state, a spectacle for all to behold.

And so it was that Henry, once a king in name, was consigned to an unmarked grave in the hallowed grounds of Chertsey, his memory eclipsed by the triumph of Edward's reign. Amidst the solemnity of his passing, whispers lingered of the true architects of his demise, of the hands that wielded the dagger and the hearts that harbored ambition.

With George, Edward's erstwhile ally and potential obstacle to Richard's ascension, standing in his path, the Duke of Gloucester saw an opportunity ripe for the plucking. But he was gone. Edward, plagued by ill health and the specter of premature death, seemed but a frail barrier between Richard and the throne, his children too young to wield the scepter of authority.

Though the Duke of Gloucester had feigned opposition to the Duke of Clarence's execution in the halls of Parliament, his silence spoke volumes, betraying his true intentions. For when the opportunity arose to intercede on behalf of his brother, Richard remained ominously silent, his eyes fixed upon the prize that lay tantalizingly within his reach. And as George's estates fell into his possession, like ripe fruit falling from the tree, Richard wasted no time in laying the foundations of his power.

Two magnificent religious establishments, born from the ashes of his brother's demise, rose under Richard's patronage, their spires reaching skyward speaking volumes of his newfound wealth and influence. Amidst the grandeur of his philanthropy, there lingered a shadow of expiation, a whispered penance for sins unspoken -for the licenses granted for these foundations bore the mark of George's blood, their ink stained with the memory of his untimely demise, just three days prior.

Richard's machinations extended beyond the realm of familial intrigue, weaving a tangled web of political maneuvering. In the wake of Anne de Mowbray's passing, the question of her estates loomed large. His cunning strategy, made all her estates come under his authority, previously bestowed to the lords Howard and Berkeley. With the rightful heirs at law sidelined and their claims extinguished by the stroke of Parliament's pen, Richard emerged as the sole beneficiary of Anne's inheritance, his coffers swelling with the spoils of ambition.

In the aftermath of the Battle of Tewkesbury, Edward's wrath descended upon his enemies with merciless ferocity, staining the halls of the Abbey church with the blood of fifteen souls. Their crime? Seeking sanctuary within the church's sacred walls, their lives forfeit to Edward's unrelenting thirst for vengeance.

For Edward, the executions bore the mark of Lancastrian sympathies, a stain upon his legacy that threatened to tarnish the gleam of his triumph.

Chapter Four

In the twilight of King Edward's reign, as the specter of mortality loomed large over his once vibrant court, the seeds of discord sown amongst his closest allies threatened to cast a shadow over the future of his kingdom. Though Edward had long turned a blind eye to the tensions that simmered beneath the surface of his court, his failing health forced him to confront the reality of his mortality and the precarious state of his realm.

Edward was grappled with the weight of his responsibilities as both monarch and father, his thoughts consumed by the fate of his children and the legacy he would leave behind. With the youth of his offspring casting a shadow over the stability of the realm, Edward recognized the urgent need for unity amongst his fractious allies, lest their squabbling plunge the kingdom into chaos.

Summoning his closest advisors and kinsmen, including the Lord Marquis Dorset, Richard and Lord Hastings, Edward sought to mend the rifts that threatened to tear his court asunder. Though Dorset, the Queen's son from her previous marriage, and Hastings, the Lord Chamberlain, had long been at odds, Edward hoped to reconcile their differences for the sake of his children and the future of the realm.

Propped up by pillows, his once robust frame now weakened by illness, Edward addressed his assembled council with a solemnity befitting the gravity of the moment. His words, laden with the weight of his impending demise, carried a king's plea for unity and concord amongst his subjects.

"My Lords, my dear kinsmen and allies," Edward began, his voice filled with a mixture of resolve and urgency. "In what plight I lie, you see, and I feel. The less time I have left in this world, the more deeply am I moved to care for the state in which I leave you, for such as I leave you, such shall my children find you."

With a father's concern etched upon his features, Edward implored his council to set aside their personal grievances and petty animosities for the greater good of the realm. He spoke of the fragility of childhood, of the need for guidance and wisdom to steer his young heirs through the tumultuous waters of court intrigue and political upheaval.

"It suffices not that you all love my children," Edward continued, his gaze sweeping across the assembled nobles. "if each of you hates the other. Childhood must be maintained by men's authority, and slipper youth underpropped with elder counsel, which neither they can have but ye give it, nor ye give it if ye agree not."

In the flickering light of the council chamber, Edward's words hung heavy in the air, a solemn reminder of the stakes at hand. For amidst the grandeur of courtly splendor and the allure of power, lay the fragile foundation of a kingdom teetering on the brink of collapse.

"Great variance has there long been between you," Edward continued, his voice tinged with a note of sorrow. "not always for great causes, sometimes a thing right well intended, our misconstruction turns into worse or a small displeasure done to us, either our own affection or evil tongues aggrieves."

As Edward's words echoed through the chamber, a palpable sense of tension hung in the air, the weight of his plea bearing down upon the hearts of all who listened. For in his final hours, the king sought not vengeance nor retribution, but reconciliation and peace amongst those who had once called themselves his allies.

"For where each labors to break that the other makes and for hated of each other's person, impugns each other's counsel, there must it needs be long ere any good conclusion go forward," Edward concluded, his voice heavy with resignation. "And also while either party labors to be chief, flattery shall have more place than plain and faithful advice, of which must needs ensue the evil bringing up of the prince, whose mind in tender youth infect, shall readily fall to mischief and riot, and draw down with this noble realm to ruin, but if grace turn him to wisdom."

As Edward's words faded into the silence of the chamber, a profound sense of introspection settled over his council, their hearts heavy with the weight of his words. For in that moment, amidst the turmoil of courtly politics and personal ambition, they were reminded of the true cost of discord and the enduring power of unity in the face of adversity.

Chapter Five

In the waning days of his reign, as the specter of mortality loomed large over the once vibrant court of England, King Edward IV sought to impart one final plea for unity and reconciliation upon his assembled council.

With each word, Edward sought to impress upon his council the urgency of their task and the dire consequences of their failure. He spoke of the insidious nature of ambition and the corrosive influence of vainglory and sovereignty, warning of the dangers posed by division and variance within the ranks of his closest allies.

"For the love that I have ever borne to you, for the love that our Lord bears to us all, from this time forward, with all grievances forgotten, love each other," Edward implored, his voice filled with concern. "which I truly trust you will, if you value anything earthly, whether God or your king, affinity or kinship, this realm, your own country, or your own safety."

With a heavy heart, Edward laid himself down on his right side, his face turned towards his assembled council, their tears mingling with his own. And as the lords comforted him with as good words as they could muster, a sense of solemn resolve settled over the chamber, their hearts united by a common purpose and a shared sense of duty.

Amidst the chaos of courtly politics and personal ambition, dark forces conspired to unravel the fragile peace that Edward had sought to preserve. The Duke of Gloucester, ever the opportunist, saw in the prince's guardianship an opportunity to advance his own ambitions, laying the foundation for a web of deceit and treachery.

As Edward's final words echoed, their wisdom transcending the boundaries of time and space, there remained a glimmer of hope amidst the darkness. For in the hearts of his loyal subjects, the flame of unity burned bright. For, in the end, it was not the might of armies or the riches of nations that determined the fate of kingdoms, but the strength of the bonds that united them in common purpose and shared destiny.

In the fateful year of 1483, King Edward IV died. With the king's passing, the fragile threads that bound the realm together threatened to unravel, leaving in its wake a vacuum of power and a tangle of conflicting ambitions.

At the time of Edward's death on the 9th of April 1483, the fate of the kingdom lay in the hands of his two surviving sons: Edward V of England, aged twelve, and Richard of Shrewsbury, Duke of York, a mere nine year old lad. In accordance with tradition, the eldest son would ascend to the throne.

As news of Edward's passing reached Ludlow Castle, where the young Edward V resided, the kingdom held its breath, awaiting the inevitable succession of the new king.

Edward IV had entrusted the guardianship of his sons to his trusted brother, Richard, Duke of Gloucester, naming him Protector during the minority of his heir. Even as Richard assumed his role as protector of the realm, whispers of betrayal and intrigue swirled through the court, casting doubt upon his true intentions.

Elizabeth Woodville determined to secure her son's ascension to the throne, dispatched messengers to her brother, Earl Rivers, urging him to assemble a force in Wales and escort the young king to London for his coronation. Her designs were soon thwarted by the machinations of Richard, Duke of Gloucester, whose own ambitions and lust for power threatened to tear the kingdom apart at its seams.

The young Edward V, found himself thrust into the midst of a political maelstrom, his innocence no match for the cunning and deceit of those who sought to manipulate him for their own gain.

As days turned into weeks, the kingdom waited with bated breath for the coronation of its new king. But as the weeks stretched into months, it became clear that the path to the throne would not be an easy one for the young Edward V.

Amidst the turmoil of succession, the kingdom mourned the passing of its beloved monarch, whose reign had been marked by prosperity and peace. Edward IV, who had ruled for twenty-two years, one month, and eight days, left behind a legacy of fair issue: his sons Edward and Richard, his daughters Elizabeth, Cecily, Bridget, Anne, and Katherine.

As the kingdom mourned the passing of its king, the wheels of fate continued to turn, and Edward IV was laid to rest with great funeral honor and solemnity at Windsor. His body was interred in the grounds of the royal mausoleum.

The young princes Edward and Richard prepared to embark on their journey towards the throne.

As the sun set on the reign of Edward IV, England found itself standing on the precipice of a new era. Amidst the tumult of succession, one thing remained clear: the kingdom would never be the same again.

Chapter Six

King Edward IV was a figure of regal stature, his presence commanding reverence and admiration from all who beheld him. A man of noble bearing, with a countenance that exuded royal dignity and a heart filled with courage and wisdom. Such was the portrait painted of the late King, a monarch whose reign had been marked by both triumph and tribulation.

In his prime, the King stood as a paragon of virtue and strength, unyielding in the face of adversity and steadfast in his commitment to justice and mercy. His counsel was sought by lords and commoners alike, his words had the wisdom earned through years of experience and hardship. Though prosperous in times of plenty, he remained humble and joyful, his pride tempered by a sense of duty and humility before his subjects.

In matters of war, the King was a formidable adversary, his bravery on the battlefield matched only by his astuteness in strategy and tactics. Despite his prowess as a warrior, he was never one to seek conflict needlessly, preferring diplomacy and negotiation over bloodshed whenever possible. His wars, carefully considered and judiciously waged, his victories won not through brute force alone, but through cunning and foresight.

Physically, the King was a striking figure, possessed of a handsome countenance and a powerful physique that spoke of his martial prowess. Though in his later years he had succumbed somewhat to the pleasures of the table, his corpulence did little to diminish his imposing presence. Even in his youth, he had been prone to carnal indulgence, a weakness that had troubled him in times of prosperity had been tempered by age and experience.

During the twilight years of his reign, the realm had known a period of unparalleled peace and prosperity. External threats had been quelled, internal strife had been reconciled, and the people had lived in harmony under his benevolent rule. His subjects, both noble and common, had regarded him with a love and reverence that bordered on adoration.

In his final days, the King had sought solace in the company of his people, reaching out to them with a warmth and familiarity that endeared him to all who knew him. His kindness and generosity had reached the hearts of the common folk, who saw in him not just a ruler, but a friend and benefactor. His actions, such as inviting the Mayor and Aldermen of London to hunt and feast with him at Windsor, had endeared him to the masses, winning him their undying loyalty and affection.

And so it was that when the noble King passed away, his death left a void in the hearts of his subjects that could never be filled. His love for his people and their unwavering devotion to him had served as a fortress and armor for his noble children, shielding them from harm.

Even as his legacy endured, the seeds of division and dissension had taken root, threatening to undo all that he had worked so hard to build.

There were those who coveted the throne and would stop at nothing to seize it for themselves. The execrable desire for sovereignty had driven them to plot and scheme, their ambition blinding them to the bonds of kinship and kindness that should have united them. And in their pursuit of power, they had laid waste to all that the King had held dear, leaving his children vulnerable and defenseless in the face of their treachery.

At the age of forty-one, Earl Rivers was already recognized as one of the most accomplished noblemen of his time, possessing a rare blend of intellect, courage, and piety that set him apart from his peers.

Earl Rivers, was a man whose character was as multifaceted as the times in which he lived. Gallant yet virtuous, brave yet compassionate, Rivers was a man of contradictions, navigating the treacherous waters of court politics with grace and integrity. In an age marked by boisterousness and savageness, he remained steadfast in his commitment to honor his actions guided by a deep sense of duty to king and country.

One of Rivers' most enduring legacies was his pivotal role in introducing the noble art of printing into England. As a patron of William Caxton, the first

English printer, Rivers played a crucial role in bringing the written word to the masses, thereby contributing to the restoration of learning and culture in the kingdom. Alongside Tiptoft, Earl of Worcester, Rivers championed the cause of education and enlightenment, laying the groundwork for a new era of intellectual growth and discovery.

Yet despite his efforts to promote learning and culture, England lagged behind other nations on the continent in matters of scholarship and enlightenment. The early productions of English printers, though significant in their own right, paled in comparison to the literary treasures of their European counterparts.

But even as Rivers labored to promote the cause of learning, the kingdom found itself plunged into a maelstrom of political intrigue. In the wake of King Edward IV's untimely death, the realm was thrown into chaos, as rival factions vied for control of the throne and the future of the kingdom hung in the balance.

At the heart of the turmoil was the struggle for power between Richard, Duke of Gloucester, and the young King Edward V. If Edward ascended to the throne, Richard would be known as the Lord Protector, entrusted with the task of guiding the young monarch through the perils of his minority. Behind the facade of loyalty and duty lay a web of deceit and ambition, as Richard plotted to secure his own grip on power at any cost.

As Edward and the Duke of Gloucester made their way to London, tensions simmered beneath the surface, threatening to erupt into open conflict at any moment.

Chapter Seven

As the night wore on, a facade of friendly cheer masked the dark intentions of the Dukes and Lord Rivers. Amidst laughter and camaraderie, they shared wine and jests, the air thick with the illusion of camaraderie. Beneath the surface, a storm was brewing, unseen by the unsuspecting Lord Rivers, who retired for the night, unaware of the treachery that awaited him.

In the stillness of the night, the Dukes and their closest allies convened in council, their whispers drowned out by the darkness that enveloped them. In hushed tones, they plotted their next move, their faces set in grim determination as they laid the groundwork for their betrayal. As the first light of dawn crept over the horizon, they dispersed, sending discreet messages to their servants to prepare for departure.

In the quiet streets of Northampton, their followers hastened to obey, while Lord Rivers' own servants remained oblivious to the impending danger. Locked within the inn, their movements restricted by the keys held firmly in the Dukes' grasp, they could only watch as their masters' plans unfolded before them.

Meanwhile, on the highway to Stony Stratford, the Dukes had stationed their men, ensuring that none could leave without their consent. With every avenue of escape blocked, Lord Rivers found himself trapped, his frustration mounting as he realized the extent of his predicament. Determined not to be cowed by the machinations of his enemies, he resolved to confront them and demand answers.

The accusations hurled at Lord Richard Gray, Sir Thomas Vaughan, and Lord Rivers reverberated through the air, each word dripping with venom and suspicion. The young King, caught off guard by the sudden turn of events, stood bewildered.

In the face of these allegations, the young King remained resolute in his defense of his uncle and brother, vehemently denying any involvement in the plots laid at their feet. Yet, his protests fell on deaf ears as the Dukes of Gloucester and Buckingham pressed forward with their plans, their eyes gleaming with triumph as they seized their prey.

With the King in their custody once more, the Dukes wasted no time in asserting their dominance, dismissing those loyal to Lord Rivers and replacing them with their own trusted allies. The young King, his heart heavy with sorrow and confusion, could only watch helplessly as his world crumbled around him, his eyes filled with tears, being a silent spectator to the events that followed.

Amidst the chaos, a small gesture of kindness from the Duke of Gloucester offered a fleeting moment of solace to Lord Rivers, a dish sent from his own table with a message of comfort. Even as he savoured this small act of compassion, Lord Rivers knew that his fate had been sealed, his future now at the mercy of his captors.

As the days passed, Lord Rivers and his companions were swiftly transported to the North country, their journey marked by the heavy chains that bound them and the shadows of despair that loomed over them. In the dark confines of their prison cells, they awaited their fate with a mixture of resignation and defiance, their spirits unbroken despite the looming specter of death that hung over them.

As Lord Rivers approached, his demeanor calm and composed, the dukes wasted no time in accusing him of treachery. Despite his attempts to defend himself, he was swiftly seized and thrown into confinement, his protestations falling on deaf ears.

With their rival incapacitated, the dukes proceeded to Stony Stratford, where the young King awaited their arrival. As they dismounted and approached the royal entourage, their faces betrayed no hint of the deceit that lay behind their smiles. With feigned humility, they knelt before the King, their words laced with false piety as they pledged their allegiance.

Even as they bowed before him, their true intentions became clear. With accusations flying and tempers flaring, they turned their ire towards Lord Richard Gray, the King's brother, accusing him and his companions of treason and plotting against the crown.

Despite Richard's assurances of loyalty, his true intentions remained shrouded in secrecy, as he moved swiftly to eliminate anyone who stood in the way of his ambition. Earl Rivers, along with Edward's half-brother Richard Gray and the king's chamberlain Thomas Vaughan, were soon executed on charges of treason, their deaths striking fear into the hearts of their allies.

As the date of the ceremony drew near, the young prince found himself caught in a web of deceit and intrigue, as Richard's machinations threatened to engulf him and his kingdom in darkness.

Chapter Eight

Richard, Duke of Gloucester, cast a complex figure, his character shaped by a myriad of influences and motivations. While his actions were often shrouded in controversy and intrigue, there were those who saw in him a man driven by noble intentions and a sense of duty to his country. Despite the clouds of suspicion that surrounded him, Richard possessed a deep-rooted sense of justice and charity, traits that endeared him to many of his subjects.

Richard endeavored to prevent tyranny and uphold the principles of justice and fairness. He was known for his charitable deeds, often restoring the property of convicted men to their families and providing pensions to the wives of traitors who plotted against him. His acts of compassion and generosity bore commitment to the welfare of his people.

One of Richard's most significant undertakings was his assumption of the governance of the young King Edward V, following the death of his father, King Edward IV. With humility and reverence, Richard took upon himself the responsibility of guiding the young monarch, seeking to ensure his well-being and the stability of the realm.

The news of the arrests and disappearances of key figures in the court reached Queen Elizabeth in the dead of night, plunging her into a state of distress and despair. Her brother and her husband's friends had all been taken away, their fate uncertain and their whereabouts unknown. In a moment of anguish, the queen cursed the day she had ever advised the consolidation of power around the king, lamenting the ruin that had befallen her family and her own ill fortune.

In a desperate bid to escape the clutches of her enemies, Queen Elizabeth sought refuge in the Sanctuary, taking herself, her younger son, and her daughters to the safety of the Abbot's place. There, amidst the chaos and confusion of their hasty departure, they found solace in the sanctuary of despair, their hopes of a brighter future fading with each passing moment.

Meanwhile, the Archbishop of York, then Chancellor of England, received word of the unfolding events in the early hours of the morning. Despite assurances from the Lord Chamberlain that all would be well, the Archbishop harbored doubts and fears about the true intentions of those in power. With a heavy heart, he made his way to the Queen's side, offering what comfort and reassurance he could.

As the Archbishop sought to console the distraught queen, he spoke words of hope and encouragement, assuring her that her son's claim to the throne would prevail. With a solemn promise to crown her younger son should the need arise, he handed her the Great

Seal, a symbol of authority and legitimacy, and departed into the dawn of a new day.

In the sanctuary of the Abbey, Queen Elizabeth and her children waited, their future hanging in the balance as the forces of power and ambition clashed outside. Amidst the turmoil, they clung to the hope that justice would prevail and their rightful place in the kingdom would be restored. But as the shadows lengthened and the echoes of betrayal grew louder, they could only pray for deliverance from the storm that raged around them.

From his chamber window, overlooking the Thames, a scene of foreboding unfolded before Lord Hastings' eyes. The river teemed with boats bearing the emblem of the Duke of Gloucester. No one could pass unsearched, no one could evade the watchful eyes of Richard's men, who stood guard with unwavering vigilance.

Throughout the city, whispers of discontent swept through the streets like a gathering storm. Lords, knights, and gentlemen, torn between loyalty to the crown and fear for their own safety, congregated in hushed groups, their minds awash with speculation and doubt. Some, fueled by animosity towards Queen Elizabeth, rallied to Richard's cause, while others, gripped by apprehension, questioned the motives behind the sudden upheaval.

Just days earlier, on 5th June, the Protector had set the date for the king's coronation for the 22nd, a proclamation that had filled the realm with anticipation and excitement. Yet, in the blink of an eye, everything changed. The Lords convened in London, their deliberations shrouded in secrecy and suspicion. Sensing the weight of his own hastiness, the Archbishop of York took precautions, retrieving the Seal and carrying it with him as a symbol of his authority.

Amidst the gathering, Lord Hastings emerged as a voice of reason and reassurance with his unwavering loyalty to the king. He sought to dispel the rumors and innuendos that clouded the air, urging his fellow Lords to trust in the steadfastness of the Duke of Gloucester's allegiance to his prince. With measured words and calm conviction, he painted a picture of innocence, casting doubt upon the motives of those who had been apprehended.

Lord Hastings assured the assembly that the arrests of Lord Rivers, Lord Richard, and the other knights were not indicative of any threat to the king's safety but rather a precautionary measure against alleged plots orchestrated by the accused. He implored his peers to withhold judgment until all the facts had been laid bare, warning against the dangers of allowing private grievances to fester and divide them further.

Despite the skepticism that lingered in the air, Lord Hastings' words carried a semblance of truth, soothing the frayed nerves of those in attendance. The imminent arrival of the Dukes of Gloucester and Buckingham, accompanied by prince Edward himself, lent credence to his assurances, their presence a commitment to the royal cause.

As the procession made its way through the streets of London, rumors spread like wildfire, fueled by speculation and fear. The sight of the dukes' servants, bearing barrels purportedly filled with weapons of war, served as a chilling reminder of the alleged threat that had been averted.

Though wise men saw through the veil of deception, recognizing the improbability of such clandestine schemes, the common folk embraced with fervor. To them, the arrests and executions were a necessary measure to safeguard the realm against would-be usurpers, their punishment a fitting end to those who dared to challenge the authority of the crown.

Chapter Nine

As prince Edward's procession drew near the city, the Mayor of London, Edmund Shaa, along with the sheriffs and aldermen, gathered to receive him with all due reverence at Harnesy. Accompanied by five hundred horsemen of the city's citizens, clad in violet, they formed an impressive escort, guiding the young monarch into the heart of the bustling metropolis.

Among the throng that greeted him stood the Duke of Gloucester, his demeanor a stark contrast to the disdain with which he had been regarded mere days before. Displaying an air of humility and deference, he publicly pledged his loyalty to the prince, winning the trust and admiration of those who had once doubted his intentions. Such was the unpredictability of fate, that the lamb had been entrusted to the wolf for safekeeping, a decision fraught with peril.

At the subsequent council convened to address the affairs of the realm, the Archbishop of York, who had previously delivered the Great Seal to the Queen, faced stern reproach for his actions. The Seal was promptly reclaimed and bestowed upon Doctor Russell, Bishop of Lincoln, a man renowned for his wisdom and scholarly acumen. Various lords and knights were assigned to key positions within the council, ensuring a balance of power and authority.

Despite the protector's fervent desire to solidify his grip on the throne, he recognized the need for caution and strategic planning. Aware that deposing one brother would inevitably lead to the other assuming the mantle of power, he bided his time, waiting for the opportune moment to strike. His gaze fixed firmly on the prize, he knew that patience was key to achieving his ultimate goal.

Proposing a plan to address the lingering issue of the king's brother, who remained ensconced in sanctuary, the protector sought to portray the Queen's actions as a deliberate ploy to undermine the authority of the king's councilors. He advocated for a diplomatic approach, suggesting that an honorable emissary, such as the Cardinal, be dispatched to persuade her to relinquish custody of the young prince.

Should persuasion fail, however, the Protector made it clear that he was prepared to take more drastic measures. Asserting the king's authority, he declared his intention to retrieve the prince from sanctuary, if necessary, by force. His reasoning was twofold: to ensure the safety and welfare of the young prince, and to prevent his potential removal from the realm by those opposed to the current regime.

In his impassioned plea for reform, the Protector condemned the abuse of sanctuaries, which he argued had become havens for criminals and traitors, rather than sanctuaries for the innocent and oppressed. Calling for decisive action, he urged the council to root out corruption and uphold the sanctity of these sacred places, while acknowledging their importance in times of genuine need.

Ultimately, the Protector's proposal was met with cautious approval, as the council weighed the risks and rewards of intervening in such a delicate matter. While some voiced concerns over the potential repercussions of forcibly removing the prince from sanctuary, others saw it as a necessary step to safeguard the stability and security of the realm.

"The issue of sanctuary has long been a contentious topic, fraught with moral and legal complexities. At its core lies the question of when and under what circumstances the privilege of sanctuary should be invoked." The Duke of Gloucester, ever the shrewd statesman, seized upon this debate as an opportunity to further his own agenda.

In his impassioned plea, the Duke sought to challenge the conventional understanding of sanctuary, arguing that its purpose was not to shield individuals from lawful harm, but rather to provide refuge for those in genuine peril. Drawing upon both theological and legal precedent, he contended that the prince, being innocent of any wrongdoing and lacking the capacity to request sanctuary, had no rightful claim to its protection.

The Duke's reasoning struck a chord with many of those present, both clergy and laymen alike, who were swayed by his eloquence and logic. They questioned the necessity of sanctuary for a child who, by virtue of his tender age and royal status, appeared to be far removed from any immediate danger.

Indeed, the Duke's astute observations laid bare the inherent contradictions within the concept of sanctuary, particularly when applied to individuals who lacked the capacity to understand or consent to its terms. He argued that while sanctuary may have been intended as a safeguard against unjust persecution, it should not serve as a shield for those who had neither the wisdom to seek it nor the culpability to warrant it.

The Duke's remarks sparked a spirited debate among the assembled councilors, with some voicing support for his proposal to remove the prince from sanctuary, while others expressed reservations about the potential repercussions of such a course of action. Yet, the prevailing sentiment seemed to favor the Duke's stance, as many agreed that the prince's welfare would be best served by bringing him out of sanctuary and into the care of the royal court.

In the end, a consensus emerged among the temporal and spiritual authorities present, who concurred that if the prince remained in sanctuary despite lacking any legitimate cause for seeking refuge, then he should be forcibly removed for his own good. This pragmatic approach reflected a deeper understanding of the law, one that prioritized the well-being of the individual over abstract notions of sanctuary.

One thing remained clear: the Duke of Gloucester's skillful manipulation of the sanctuary debate had brought him one step closer to achieving his goal of consolidating power and securing the throne for himself.

Chapter Ten

The Lord Cardinal was summoned to take up the role of convincing the queen to release her younger son, Richard. As the Lord Cardinal and his accompanying lords awaited the Queen's response within the confines of the sanctuary, the tension in the air was palpable.

With a mix of diplomacy and maternal concern, the Queen addressed the council's request. She acknowledged the importance of reuniting the royal brothers and recognized the benefits of having them together in the king's court. Yet, she also expressed her reservations, rooted in the health and well-being of her youngest son, the Duke of York.

"My lords," she began, her voice measured yet firm, "I do not deny the convenience of having the young prince in the company of his brother, the King. However, I must emphasize the delicate state of his health, which requires constant care and attention. He has recently been afflicted by a severe illness, from which he has only begun to recover. As his mother, I am best suited to provide him with the care he needs, as I have done since his birth."

The Queen's words carried a sense of maternal and protective instinct. She argued that despite the benefits of reuniting the royal brothers, the Duke of York's fragile health made it imperative for him to remain under her care, at least for the time being. Her concerns were not unfounded, as the health of the young prince was indeed a matter of utmost importance, given the precarious nature of his recovery.

The Lord Cardinal listened intently, weighing the Queen's words against the council's concerns. He recognized the validity of her points, yet also understood the broader implications of her decision. It was not simply a matter of familial duty, but also a question of political expediency and royal protocol.

Responding to the Queen's concerns, the Lord Cardinal sought to reassure her that her son's well-being would be safeguarded, even outside the sanctuary. He emphasized the importance of family unity and the benefits of having the royal brothers together, both for their personal development and for the stability of the kingdom.

"Your grace," he said respectfully, "I understand your concerns for the health of your son, and I assure you that his well-being will be a top priority for all concerned. However, it is also important to consider the broader interests of the realm. The presence of the Duke of York at court would not only be a source of comfort to his brother, the King, but also a symbol of unity and strength for the kingdom."

The Lord Cardinal's words were carefully chosen, intended to assuage the Queen's fears while also gently urging her to consider the greater good. He recognized the delicate balance between maternal instinct and political necessity, and sought to navigate it with tact and diplomacy.

As the discussion continued, other members of the council weighed in, offering their perspectives on the matter. Some echoed the Lord Cardinal's sentiments, emphasizing the importance of family unity and the benefits of having the royal brothers together. Others, however, expressed sympathy for the Queen's concerns, acknowledging the challenges of balancing familial duty with political obligation.

As the debate within the sanctuary chamber intensified, the Queen remained resolute in her position, determined to protect her son, and uphold the sanctity of the sanctuary. Despite the Cardinal's attempts to persuade her otherwise, she steadfastly refused to yield to the pressure exerted by the council.

The Cardinal, recognizing the Queen's unwavering resolve, attempted to address her concerns. He assured her that the safety of her kin and herself was not in jeopardy, and that the council had no intention of causing her harm. Yet, the Queen remained skeptical, wary of the motives behind the council's actions and distrustful of their intentions.

"Why should I trust in the assurances of those who have shown no regard for justice or fairness?" the Queen questioned, her voice tinged with bitterness. "They seek to paint me as a villain, to cast doubt upon my innocence and loyalty. But I know their true intentions, and I will not be swayed by their deceitful words."

The Cardinal, taken aback by the Queen's defiance, sought to reason with her, appealing to her sense of duty and responsibility as a mother and a queen. He reminded her of the importance of family unity and the need for her son to be with his brother, the king. The Queen remained unmoved, her maternal instincts overriding any sense of duty or obligation to the crown.

"It is not for them to dictate where my son should be," the Queen declared, her voice ringing with determination. "He is under my care, and I will not relinquish him to those who seek to harm him. Let them come and try to take him if they dare, but they will find that I will not yield so easily."

Her heart heavy with the burden of responsibility, she knew that she could no longer cling to the sanctuary's protection, no matter how fiercely she desired to shield her child from harm.

In her mind's eye, the Queen replayed the memories of her past struggles and triumphs within the walls of sanctuary. She recalled the birth of her eldest son, now who would be the king, and the joy and relief she felt when he was safely cradled in her arms. Sanctuary had been her refuge in times of peril, her haven of safety amidst the storm of political intrigue.

Yet now, faced with the prospect of relinquishing her youngest son to the care of others, the Queen was dealing with conflicting emotions within herself. On one hand, her maternal instinct urged her to hold onto her child with all her strength, to protect him at any cost. On the other hand, she knew that she could not keep him hidden away forever, that eventually, he would need to emerge from the sanctuary's protective embrace and face the challenges of the world beyond.

The Cardinal, realizing that further attempts to persuade the Queen would be futile, reluctantly conceded defeat. He knew that he could not force her hand, and that any attempt to do so would only further alienate her from the council. With a heavy heart, he bid the Queen farewell and departed from the sanctuary, leaving her to face the challenges ahead alone.

As the Queen watched the Cardinal and his retinue depart, she felt a sense of pride and defiance swell within her. She knew that she had stood her ground against those who sought to undermine her authority, and that she had upheld the honor and dignity of her family. Though the road ahead would be fraught with challenges and dangers, she remained undaunted, confident in her ability to protect her son.

As she looked upon her son, nestled safely in her arms, she knew that she would do whatever it took to ensure his safety and well-being. For in the end, her love for him was stronger than any threat or obstacle that the council could throw her way. And with that thought in mind, she drew him close, determined to face whatever trials lay ahead with courage and defiance.

As the Lord Cardinal and his companions departed the sanctuary, they did so with a sense of resignation. Though they had hoped to persuade the Queen to relinquish custody of her son, they respected her decision and understood the depth of her maternal devotion.

Chapter Eleven

The Protector, the Duke of Gloucester was resolute in his determination to bring the younger prince out of the sanctuary. He commanded the Cardinal to summon the younger son of the Queen and if he was not able to, obviously he would be taking the most unfavourable step of getting to the prince by brutal force.

The atmosphere in the Star Chamber at Westminster was fraught with tension as the Lord Cardinal prepared to embark on his delicate mission to persuade the Queen to relinquish custody of the young prince, a second time. The councilors, gathered solemnly, understood the necessity of handling it with the utmost care to avoid any hint of scandal or controversy.

The Lord Cardinal, accompanied by several other lords, including trusted advisors and members of the council, made his way towards the sanctuary where the Queen resided with her younger son. Their purpose was clear: to appeal to her sense of reason and duty, and to convince her that it was in the best interest of all parties involved for the prince to be reunited with his brother, the king.

As they entered the sanctuary, the Lord Cardinal keenly observed the Queen's demeanor, noting any signs of resistance or reluctance that might complicate their negotiations. It was crucial that she understood the implications of her decision, both for the well-being of her family and for the stability of the realm.

Upon meeting with the Queen, the Lord Cardinal addressed her with a mixture of diplomacy and firmness, expressing the concerns of the council and the broader implications of her actions. He emphasized the importance of family unity and the need for the young prince to be brought into the king's presence, where he could be properly cared for and educated according to his station.

The Lord Cardinal framed the request as not only a matter of royal protocol but also as a gesture of goodwill towards the king and the realm at large. He appealed to the Queen's sense of duty as a mother and as a member of the royal family, urging her to consider the greater good above all else.

In making his case, the Lord Cardinal also sought to assuage any fears or reservations the Queen might have about relinquishing custody of her son. He assured her that the prince would be treated with the utmost respect and care, and that his welfare would be a top priority for all concerned. Moreover, he emphasized the importance of the prince's presence at court, where he could receive the education and upbringing befitting his royal status.

As the Lord Cardinal spoke, the other lords present lent their support, reinforcing his arguments. They emphasized the practical benefits of reuniting the royal brothers, highlighting the potential for greater stability and harmony within the realm.

Throughout the meeting, the Lord Cardinal remained vigilant, carefully gauging the Queen's reaction and adjusting his approach accordingly. He was mindful of the delicate balance between persuasion and coercion, knowing that any hint of forcefulness could backfire and alienate the Queen further.

As the Cardinal pressed her for a final decision, the Queen felt a surge of determination course through her veins. She knew that she could not allow her own fears and doubts to cloud her judgment, that she must act in the best interests of her son, even if it meant letting him go.

In the end, the Lord Cardinal's efforts proved successful, as the Queen agreed to release custody of the young Duke into the care of the council. Her decision was not made lightly, but rather out of a sense of duty and a recognition of the broader implications of her actions.

With a heavy heart and tear-filled eyes, the Queen took her son by the hand and turned to the lords assembled before her. In a voice choked with emotion, she entrusted them with the care and protection of her beloved child, placing her faith in their honor and integrity.

"I trust you with the life of my son," she whispered, her voice trembling with emotion. "Guard him well, for he is the future of our kingdom, the hope of our people. May God watch over him and keep him safe from harm."

As the Queen released her grip on her son's hand, she felt a sense of profound loss wash over her. In that moment, she knew that she was sacrificing not only her son's safety but also a part of herself.

However, she also knew that this sacrifice was necessary, that it was the price she must pay to ensure her son's future and the stability of the realm. And so, with a heavy heart and a silent prayer on her lips, she watched as her son was led away by the lords, his fate now in their hands.

With the prince's release secured, the Lord Cardinal and his companions departed the sanctuary, their mission accomplished. As they returned to the Star Chamber, there was a palpable sense of relief and satisfaction among the councilors, knowing that they had averted a potential crisis and secured the unity of the royal family.

As the echoes of their footsteps faded into the distance, the Queen sank to her knees, her tears mingling with the dust of the sanctuary floor. In that moment of solitude and despair, she found solace in the knowledge that she had done everything in her power to protect her son.

And as she gazed up at the heavens above, she whispered a silent prayer, a prayer for her son's safety and well-being, a prayer for the future of the kingdom, a prayer for peace and justice to prevail in a kingdom torn apart by greed and ambition.

For in that moment, the Queen knew that her sacrifice had not been in vain, that her love for her son had transcended the boundaries of sanctuary and reached out into the world beyond. And though she hoped to see him again, as often as she could, she would carry his memory in her heart.

In the days that followed, the young prince was brought to court, where he was welcomed with open arms and treated with the respect and reverence befitting his royal status. His reunion with his brother, the king, was a moment of great joy and celebration, symbolizing the strength and resilience of the monarchy.

The Lord Cardinal's skillful diplomacy and persuasive eloquence had played a crucial role in resolving the crisis, earning him the gratitude and admiration of his peers. His efforts had not only secured the prince's release but had also reaffirmed the bonds of loyalty and allegiance that bound the realm together.

As the Lord Cardinal reflected on the events that had transpired, he knew that the challenges facing the monarchy were far from over. Yet, he also took comfort in the knowledge that with unity and resolve, the royal family would weather any storm and emerge stronger than ever before. And as long as he stood by their side, guiding them with wisdom and foresight, he was confident that they would overcome whatever obstacles lay ahead.

Chapter Twelve

Richard, Duke of Gloucester, was a man consumed by ambition, willing to sacrifice anything and anyone to achieve his goals. Central to Richard's plans were two men of honor and influence: Edward, Duke of Buckingham, and Lord Hastings. Both held significant power within the realm, the former through his distinguished ancestry and the latter through his close ties to the king. Despite their mutual animosity, fueled by years of political intrigue and rivalry, they shared a common enemy in the Queen's faction, whom they viewed as a threat to their own interests.

Under the guise of avenging old grievances and settling scores, Richard manipulated the simmering tensions between the Queen's kin and the king's blood. He cunningly exploited their divisions, knowing that their mutual distrust and animosity would pave the way for his own rise to power. By fanning the flames of discord and sowing seeds of mistrust, Richard set the stage for the destruction of his enemies and the consolidation of his own power.

With Buckingham and Hastings at his side, Richard orchestrated a plot to eliminate the Queen's allies from the king's inner circle, branding them as enemies of the crown. Under the pretext of protecting the king from perceived threats, Richard persuaded the Queen to keep the young monarch away from the court, thereby isolating him from his mother's influence and ensuring his own control over the royal household.

Richard's machinations did not end there. Sensing an opportunity to exploit the king's absence for his own gain, he secretly plotted to seize the throne for himself, knowing that the lords who remained with the king would be powerless to oppose him without the support of their allies. With cunning and guile, Richard laid the groundwork for his own coronation, carefully maneuvering behind the scenes to ensure that his rivals would be powerless to stop him.

But Richard's ambitions were not without risk. His actions had alienated many within the realm, and rumors of his treachery had begun to spread. Yet, undeterred by the whispers of dissent, Richard pressed forward with his plans, confident in his ability to outmaneuver his enemies and secure his grip on the throne.

As the Lord Cardinal and the other lords received the young Duke from the Queen's reluctant embrace, they found themselves caught in the tangled web of political intrigue that had gripped the kingdom. With the boy now in their custody, they knew that they held in their hands not only the future of the monarchy but also the balance of power within the realm.

They escorted the young Duke to the Protector, whose welcoming embrace belied the machinations brewing beneath the surface. With calculated grace, the

Protector greeted the boy, masking his true intentions behind a facade of warmth and hospitality. From there, they ushered him to his brother, the monarch-to-be.

Together, they made their way to the Tower, where they would remain in the shadow of its imposing walls, shielded from prying eyes and whispered rumors.

With promises of marriage alliances and other rewards, the Protector and the Duke conspired to seize the throne, their ambitions overshadowing any semblance of loyalty or honor.

As preparations for the young King's coronation continued apace, the Lords convened in the Tower to discuss the arrangements. The air crackled with tension as they debated the finer points of protocol and tradition, their minds consumed by thoughts of power and prestige.

But amidst the hustle and bustle of their deliberations, a shadow fell over the proceedings, casting a pall of uncertainty over the gathered assembly. It was the Protector who entered the chamber, his demeanor a curious blend of charm and calculation. With practiced ease, he greeted the Lords, apologizing for his absence and attributing it to a brief respite.

Behind the facade of geniality, a storm brewed within him, his mind racing with thoughts of treachery. His eyes darted from face to face, searching for signs of dissent or disloyalty, while his lips curled into a thin smile that failed to reach his eyes.

Turning to the Bishop of Ely, he remarked casually on the delicious strawberries in the bishop's garden, a seemingly innocuous comment that belied the sinister intent lurking beneath the surface. With a sly grin, he requested a serving of the succulent fruit, his appetite whetted by the prospect of indulgence.

The bishop, eager to please, readily agreed, offering to send his servant to fetch a dish of strawberries. But as the moments stretched into minutes, a sense of unease settled over the chamber, the air thick with anticipation and foreboding.

An hour passed, and the Protector returned to the chamber, his demeanor markedly changed. Gone was the mask of geniality, replaced instead by a dark cloud of anger and resentment. His brows furrowed in consternation, his lips pressed into a thin line of discontent as he took his seat among the assembled Lords.

In the silence that followed, a sense of unease descended upon the chamber, the tension palpable as the Lords exchanged uneasy glances. Something had shifted in the Protector's demeanor, something dark and foreboding that hinted at the storm to come.

Chapter Thirteen

Lord Hastings, in particular, was no stranger to the temptations of corruption, having shamelessly accepted bribes from both Louis XI and the Duke of Burgundy. His dealings with these foreign powers had tainted his reputation, but they had also enriched his coffers and secured his position within the council. Hastings remained a formidable adversary, his political acumen matched only by his ruthless determination to protect his own interests.

As murmurs of dissent spread through the ranks of the council, Hastings and Morton began to meet in secret, forming an unlikely alliance with members of the Woodville faction who shared their disdain for the Protector. Together, they plotted to undermine his authority and thwart his plans for the succession.

But their conspiracy did not go unnoticed by the Protector, whose spies and informants kept him apprised of every whisper and rumor within the council chambers. Sensing a threat to his power, the Protector ordered troops to be summoned from York, ready to crush any resistance with swift and decisive force.

Despite their best efforts to conceal their intentions, the conspirators' plans were soon laid bare, thanks to a timely warning from one of their own. Acting on this intelligence, the Protector moved swiftly with an intention to arrest Lord Hastings and break up the conspiracy before it could gain any further momentum.

Hastings, ever the cunning strategist, had worked tirelessly to sow discord within the council, using his influence to undermine the Woodville faction and bolster his own position. In his haste to seize power, he had underestimated the Protector's resolve and determination to crush any opposition to his rule.

As Richard urged Catesby to subtly test Lord Hastings' allegiance to their cause, the tension within their clandestine circle reached a boiling point.

Catesby, tasked with the delicate mission, approached Lord Hastings with caution, his words carefully chosen to gauge the Lord Chamberlain's stance. However, what he discovered was not what he expected. Lord Hastings stood firm, his words resolute and his loyalty unwavering. He spoke sternly, a pillar of strength amidst the swirling currents of uncertainty.

Indeed, the Lord Chamberlain's steadfastness only served to deepen the Protector's suspicions. If Lord Hastings could not be swayed, then he posed a threat to their fragile alliance. Fearful that their actions might jeopardize Lord Hastings' trust, upon which their entire plan depended, the Protector made a fateful decision: Lord Hastings must be eliminated.

But it was not only fear that drove the Protector to action. There was also the allure of power, the tantalizing prospect of seizing control over the vast resources and influence that Lord Hastings wielded in his county. It was a prize too tempting to resist.

Lord Hastings, depicted as a figure of authority alongside his prince, cast a formidable shadow over the realm. His plain and open manner to his enemies belied a shrewdness and cunning that made him a force to be reckoned with. Yet, beneath his steely exterior, beat the heart of a man of honor and courage, unafraid to face the dangers that lay ahead.

The Protector eliminated Lord Hastings, with a clap of his hands and the execution was swiftly carried out.

News of Lord Hastings' death spread like wildfire through the city, igniting a blaze of unrest. Rumors swirled, whispers of treachery and betrayal echoing through the streets. The once-beloved Lord Chamberlain had fallen, his demise sending shockwaves through the kingdom.

To mitigate the growing unrest, the Protector hastily summoned men to the Tower, donning old, ill-fitting armor to imply urgency. He spun a tale of conspiracy, weaving a web of deceit to conceal his own culpability in Lord Hastings' demise. He claimed that the Lord Chamberlain and others had conspired against him and the Duke of Buckingham, their intentions nefarious and their allegiance dubious.

But the Protector's machinations did little to quell the rising tide of suspicion and mistrust. His hastily crafted proclamation, issued in the King's name, accused Lord Hastings and his supposed co-conspirators of treason, painting them as power-hungry traitors intent on plunging the realm into chaos. As the Protector's grip on power tightened, those who dared to defy him found themselves cast aside, their lives forfeit in the ruthless game of politics that played out behind closed doors.

Chapter Fourteen

On the very day that the Lord Chamberlain met his end in the Tower of London, his comrades-in-arms suffered a similar fate at Pontefract, their heads severed from their bodies without trial or due process.

It was a grim spectacle, orchestrated by the Protector and his council, who saw an opportunity to seize power swiftly, before resistance could be organized. With the elimination of the Lord Chamberlain and his allies, they believed they could present themselves as saviors of the realm, protecting it from the machinations of a corrupt and decadent court. But to do so, they needed the support of the people, and so they turned to Edmund Shaa, the Mayor of London, and other influential figures to sway public opinion in their favor.

Their efforts did not end there. They also sought the support of spiritual leaders, whose sermons praised the Protector and his actions, filling the hearts of the faithful with adulation and reverence. It was a strategy as cunning as it was repugnant, using the pulpit to spread propaganda and manipulate the minds of the masses.

But perhaps the most audacious aspect of their plan was the pretext they concocted to depose the prince and crown the Protector in his stead. It centered around the allegation of bastardy in King Edward or his children, a claim that would invalidate their claim to the throne and pave the way for the Protector's ascension. While openly accusing King Edward risked insulting the Protector's own mother, implying bastardy in his children was a far more insidious tactic, one that struck at the heart of his legitimacy.

To lend credence to their claim, they referenced past events surrounding King Edward's marriage, weaving a web of half-truths and innuendo to support their cause. It was a calculated gamble, one that relied on the ignorance and gullibility of the masses to succeed.

Meanwhile, the council had originally hoped for an immediate coronation to avoid the need for a protectorate, drawing inspiration from historical precedents such as Richard II and Henry VI. Both monarchs had ascended the throne at a young age, yet their reigns had been marked by turmoil and instability, leading many to question the wisdom of placing power in tahe hands of a minor.

As the council grappled with the question of succession, a bombshell revelation threatened to upend the delicate balance of power within the realm. Robert Stillington, Bishop of Bath and Wells, stepped forward to reveal a long-concealed secret: that King Edward IV had been secretly married to Lady Eleanor Talbot before his union with Elizabeth Woodville.

This revelation began to cast doubt on the legitimacy of King Edward V's claim to the throne. For if Edward IV's marriage to Lady Eleanor was valid, then his subsequent marriage to Elizabeth Woodville would be deemed illegitimate, and their children would be branded as bastards, with no rightful claim to the crown.

In the shadow of Saint Paul's Cross, Stillington delivered a sermon, his words a damning indictment of the legitimacy of the House of York. With each syllable that fell from his lips, the foundations of Edward IV's reign crumbled, his once unassailable legacy tarnished by the specter of illegitimacy.

The Protector seized upon the opportunity, using the chaos and confusion to solidify his grip on power.

Amidst the tumultuous currents of court intrigue, Bishop Robert Stillington emerged as a figure of both piety and political prowess. Known for his devout adherence to the white rose cause, Stillington's influence extended far beyond the walls of his cathedral, shaping the very fabric of political discourse in the realm. His philanthropic endeavors, including the establishment of a collegiate chapel and the provision of free education, endeared him to the populace and solidified his reputation as a man of noble character.

Yet, it was not merely Bishop Robert Stillington's philanthropy that earned him renown, but his role as a key player in the unfolding drama of succession. Though he bore witness to Edward IV's secret marriage to Lady Eleanor Butler, he chose to keep this knowledge hidden until the opportune moment arose.

For Stillington understood that timing was everything in this ruthless game of power.

When the necessity finally arose, Stillington stepped forward with courage and conviction, presenting the evidence of Edward IV's previous marriage to the council. With instruments, proctors, and notaries of the law at his side, he laid bare the truth before the assembled lords, setting in motion a chain of events that would alter the course of ascension. For in that moment, the legitimacy of Edward IV's children was called into question, casting a shadow of doubt over the very foundation of the House of York.

Questioning the legitimacy of Edward IV's children and promoting the Protector's claim to the throne, Stillington's words struck at the very heart of the realm's stability, sowing seeds of doubt and discord among the populace. Yet, despite his best efforts, the Protector's attempt to stage a dramatic entrance during the sermon failed miserably, casting doubt on the sincerity of his intentions and undermining the sermon's intended impact.

As the dust settled and the echoes of Stillington's sermon faded into the ether, the realm stood on a delicate precipice.

Chapter Fifteen

The Duke of Buckingham emerged as a master of rhetoric and persuasion, wielding his words like a skilled swordsman on the battlefield of public opinion. Addressing the citizens of London with a mixture of eloquence and conviction, Buckingham sought to rally support for the Protector's claim to the throne, casting himself as a champion of justice and stability in a time of turmoil.

With every word, Buckingham painted a vivid picture of the past injustices suffered under the previous regime, appealing to the collective memory of the citizens and invoking a sense of righteous indignation at the corruption and tyranny that had plagued the realm. By framing the Protector's ascension as a necessary corrective to these past wrongs, Buckingham sought to position himself and his allies as agents of change and progress, promising relief from the instability and oppression of the past.

But Buckingham's rhetoric was not merely about pointing out the failings of the past; it was also about offering a vision of a brighter future, one in which the realm would be governed by a just and virtuous ruler who had the best interests of the people at heart. By extolling the virtues of the Protector and emphasizing his rightful claim to the throne, Buckingham sought to inspire confidence and trust among the citizens, persuading them to throw their support behind the Protector's cause.

Central to Buckingham's argument was the question of legitimacy, a topic that had been a source of contention and debate in the realm. By calling into question the legitimacy of Edward IV's children and promoting the Protector's claim as the lawful heir to the throne, Buckingham sought to undermine any lingering doubts or objections that might stand in the way of the Protector's ascension. Drawing on legal precedent and theological argumentation, Buckingham made a compelling case for the Protector's right to rule, appealing to both reason and faith in his bid to sway public opinion.

Yet, for all his rhetorical skill and persuasive prowess, Buckingham knew that words alone would not be enough to secure victory. He understood the importance of action and mobilization, of turning words into deeds and rallying support behind a common cause. Thus, he called upon the citizens of London to join him in petitioning the Protector to take on the governance of the realm, urging them to show their intentions and demonstrate their readiness to embrace change.

In doing so, Buckingham sought to harness the collective power of the people, to turn their goodwill and support into a force to be reckoned with. For he knew that in the game of politics, numbers mattered, and that the voice of the people could be a potent weapon in the hands of those who knew how to wield it. And so, with his words ringing in their ears and his vision of a brighter future beckoning them forward, the citizens of London stood at crossroads.

As the Duke of Buckingham stood before the citizens of London, his words hanging in the air, he anticipated a chorus of approval, the resounding cry of "King Richard, King Richard" ringing out from the crowd. Yet, to his astonishment, there was only silence, a profound stillness that seemed to envelop the hall like a shroud.

Confusion etched itself upon the duke's face as he turned to the mayor and other members of the council, seeking an explanation for the unexpected lack of response. Perhaps, he reasoned, the people did not fully comprehend his proposal, and so he resolved to restate it in clearer terms, with even greater eloquence and persuasion.

With a voice that was both commanding and graceful, the duke once again presented his proposal to the crowd, his words flowing like honey, sweet and enticing. Yet, despite his best efforts, the silence persisted, unbroken and unyielding.

It was then that the mayor intervened, suggesting that the people were accustomed to being addressed by the recorder, the official spokesperson for the city. And so, Fitzwilliams, the recorder, reluctantly stepped forward to repeat the duke's words, his voice echoing through the hall with solemnity and gravitas.

But still, the silence held sway, stubborn and immovable, as if the very walls themselves were conspiring against the duke's efforts. It was a silence that spoke volumes, a collective hesitation that hung heavy in the air, pregnant with unspoken thoughts and unvoiced concerns.

Undeterred, the duke turned once more to the people, his tone one of earnest pleading and genuine concern. He implored them to consider the proposal before them, emphasizing its importance for their welfare and honor. And yet, the silence persisted, unyielding in its refusal to be broken.

Then, from the lower end of the hall, a faint murmur began to rise, like the distant buzzing of bees on a summer's day. It grew louder and more insistent, until suddenly, a group of the duke's supporters, along with some eager apprentices and youths, broke into a joyous cry of "King Richard! King Richard!"

For a moment, the hall was filled with the sound of their voices, echoing off the walls in jubilant exclamation. But even as they shouted their approval, the majority of the crowd remained silent, their faces depicting a mixture of surprise and uncertainty.

Yet, in that brief moment of cacophony, the duke and the mayor seized upon the opportunity, declaring it a splendid and joyful cry to hear, a clear indication of the people's support for the duke's proposal. And with that, the silence was finally broken, as the crowd, swayed by the enthusiasm of the duke's supporters, joined in the cry of "King Richard! King Richard!"

It was a moment of triumph for the duke, a validation of his persuasive powers and his ability to rally support behind his cause.

Chapter Sixteen

As the Duke of Buckingham's words hung in the air, resonating with the weight of their collective desire, a somber mood settled over the assembled company. Some wore a facade of cheerfulness, masking the turmoil within, while others could not hide the sorrow etched upon their faces.

The following day dawned, heralding the arrival of a momentous occasion. The mayor, accompanied by the aldermen and chief commoners of the city, gathered together, resplendent in their finest attire, ready to embark on their journey to Baynard's Castle, the residence of the Lord Protector.

Alongside them marched the Duke of Buckingham, flanked by a retinue of noble men and knights, their presence adding weight and dignity to the procession. It was a scene of grandeur and solemnity, as they made their way through the bustling streets of London towards their destination.

Upon reaching Baynard's Castle, the duke dispatched word to the Lord Protector, informing him of the distinguished company gathered outside, eager to discuss an important matter of state. Yet, the Protector hesitated, wary of their sudden and unexpected visit, unsure of their intentions.

Sensing the Protector's reluctance, the Duke of Buckingham sought to reassure him, conveying the earnestness of their purpose to the mayor and others. A message was sent forth, expressing their affection and requesting permission to present their intent directly to the protector himself.

Finally, after much deliberation, the Protector emerged from his chamber, though he remained aloof, observing the assembly from a gallery above. It was a cautious approach, indicative of his wariness towards the unfolding events.

With the Protector's reluctant acquiescence, the Duke of Buckingham stepped forward, humbly petitioning on behalf of all present for forgiveness and license to state their purpose without incurring his displeasure.

Granted permission to speak, the Duke proceeded to boldly present their intent and reasons, urging the Protector to assume the crown for the welfare of the realm. He spoke of lawful rights and unanimous support, painting a compelling picture of a realm in need of a strong and capable leader.

The Protector listened intently; his expression conflicted as he was weighing their proposal. In the face of overwhelming consensus and the fervent desire for change, the Protector relented, agreeing to their request, and accepting the crown. It was a moment of profound significance, as the assembly erupted into a chorus of "Richard, King Richard," heralding the dawn of a new era.

With the proclamation of Richard III as king, the people dispersed, their minds abuzz with conversation and debate. Opinions varied, ranging from jubilation to apprehension, as they considered the implications of this moment.

For some, it was a cause for celebration, a glimmer of hope. For others, it was a portent of darker days ahead, as they pondered the consequences of placing their trust in a new and untested ruler.

The events leading up to Richard's coronation were marked by a series of calculated moves, each designed to consolidate his power and legitimize his claim to the crown. The stage for Richard's ascent was set with the death of his brother, King Edward IV, leaving behind a vacuum of leadership and a tangled web of succession disputes.

Richard wasted no time in positioning himself as the rightful heir to the throne, leveraging his influence within the Regency Council to cast doubt upon the legitimacy of Edward's marriage to Elizabeth Woodville. By branding the union as a case of bigamy, Richard sought to invalidate the second marriage and, by extension, delegitimize the offspring of the union, thereby clearing the path for his own ascension.

One of Richard's first acts of assertion was the public display of his pardon to all offenses against him, a strategic maneuver aimed at winning over various factions of society and projecting an image of magnanimity and benevolence. This gesture, coupled with his willingness to pardon even his enemies, served to bolster his image as a just and merciful ruler, earning him favor among the populace.

However, Richard's path to power was not without its obstacles, chief among them being his need to eliminate potential threats to his reign. This necessitated the swift and decisive removal of adversaries, whose allegiance to the Woodvilles posed a significant challenge to Richard's authority. By orchestrating the arrest and subsequent execution of these people in power, Richard effectively neutralized opponents, sending a chilling message to anyone who dared to oppose him.

The execution of Lord Hastings was not merely an act of retribution but a calculated move to suppress any evidence of collusion between him and the Woodvilles, thereby justifying Richard's actions and reinforcing his position as the rightful guardian of the realm. With Hastings out of the picture, Richard turned his attention to other potential threats, including members of the Woodville family, whom he deemed necessary to eliminate in order to solidify his grip on power.

With his rivals dispatched and their supporters cowed into submission, Richard moved swiftly to consolidate his hold on the throne, proclaiming himself the rightful successor to King Edward IV.

The path to Richard's coronation was paved with legal maneuverings and political machinations aimed at legitimizing his claim to the throne. The declaration of Edward and Richard as illegitimate heirs, coupled with the assertion of Richard's own legitimacy by an assembly of Lords and Commons, served to cement his position as the rightful monarch of England.

The coronation of Richard III on July 6th marked the culmination of his long and arduous journey to power, solidifying his status as the undisputed ruler of the realm.

Chapter Seventeen

The Tower of London, with its ominous silhouette looming over the River Thames, had long been shrouded in tales of intrigue and dark deeds. Yet, perhaps none seemed as haunting as the mystery surrounding the fate of Edward V, King of England, and his younger brother Richard, Duke of York. Sent to the Tower by their uncle, King Richard III, in mid-1483, the young princes vanish from public view, leaving behind a trail of speculation and conjecture.

Initially held in the "inner apartments" of the Tower, the princes were occasionally glimpsed in the garden, but as the summer of 1483 gave way to autumn, they faded from sight altogether. Their disappearance coincided with ominous reports from a visiting doctor, John Argentine, who noted Edward's increasing sense of foreboding, as if he were "like a victim prepared for sacrifice". The young prince sought solace in daily confession and penance, depicting an impending doom that loomed over the Tower.

The rebellion against Richard III in 1483, fueled in part by the desire to rescue the princes from their captivity, took a dramatic turn with the involvement of the Duke of Buckingham. With Buckingham's support, the focus shifted from a mere rescue mission to the backing of Henry Tudor, a rival claimant to the throne.

Efforts to liberate the princes from the Tower met with failure, further deepening the mystery surrounding their fate.

The whereabouts of the princes remained a subject of speculation, with rumors swirling of their possible survival as late as July 1484.

While Richard was away from court on a progression through the Yorkist heartlands at the time the princes vanished, the Tower of London, where they were held, was firmly under his control.

Richard, now king, engaged in a clandestine discussion with Sir James Tyrrell, a trusted knight in his service, regarding a "treacherous matter". Unfazed by the king's ominous request, Tyrrell accepted the task entrusted to him and was dispatched to the Tower with a letter commanding the surrender of all keys for one fateful night.

The young princes, were left under the care of a single attendant, William Slaughter, ominously nicknamed "Black Will". As night descended, Sir James Tyrrell, aided by accomplices Miles Forest and John Dighton, executed Richard's sinister decree.

Sir James Tyrrell, carried out the heinous deed upon the king's orders.

There was a dispute over land inheritance, with the ambitious Duke of Buckingham daring to challenge Richard's authority. There was a deeper rift born of envy and resentment, as the king struggled to reconcile his own aspirations with the burgeoning power of his uncle.

The tensions between Richard and Buckingham simmered beneath the surface, erupting into open animosity as the Protector's coronation approached. The duke, feigning illness to avoid accompanying Richard through the streets of London, further strained their already fragile relationship. Richard, sensing a personal slight, accused Buckingham of acting out of spite, deepening the rift between them.

Chapter Eighteen

Upon returning to Brecknock, the Duke of Buckingham found himself ensnared in the web of Bishop Morton's cunning machinations. A man of wit and wisdom, Bishop Morton was a master manipulator, adept at using his influence to further his own ends. With the duke as his unwitting pawn, Bishop Morton set about weaving a tangled web of deceit and betrayal that would ultimately lead to the duke's downfall.

At first, their relationship appeared to be one of mutual respect and camaraderie, with Bishop Morton subtly exploiting the duke's occasional displays of envy towards King Richard's glory to further his own agenda. With a keen understanding of human nature, Bishop Morton skillfully stoked the fires of the duke's ambition, all the while appearing to follow his lead. Yet, beneath the facade of friendship lay a foundation of distrust and manipulation, as Bishop Morton carefully plotted his next move.

In a private audience with the duke, Bishop Morton revealed his true intentions, casting himself as a faithful servant of King Edward IV and expressing his desire to see the rightful heir ascend the throne. His words, carefully crafted to appeal to the duke's sense of duty and honor, struck a chord with the ambitious nobleman, who eagerly sought the bishop's counsel.

As their conversation turned to matters of kingship and succession, Bishop Morton artfully danced around the topic, sharing tales and parables to illustrate his point without incriminating himself. The duke, ever eager for guidance, encouraged the bishop to speak freely, assuring him that his words would be kept in confidence.

However, as their discussion delved deeper into the murky waters of politics, Bishop Morton grew cautious, warning the duke of the dangers of meddling in matters beyond his control. He shared the cautionary tale of the lion and the horned beast, a fable that served as a thinly veiled metaphor for the perils of ambition and the consequences of overreaching.

Despite the bishop's warnings, the duke remained undeterred, his ambition fueled by the tantalizing prospect of power and influence. Yet, unbeknownst to him, Bishop Morton had already set the wheels of fate in motion, manipulating events behind the scenes to ensure the duke's downfall.

Contrary to the popular image of a ruthless and power-hungry tyrant, the real Richard III was not previously steeped in crime. He was raised amidst the tumult of the Wars of the Roses, where loyalty and betrayal were the currency of the realm. From a young age, Richard demonstrated unwavering loyalty to his brother, King Edward IV, and showed no signs of the malevolence that would later be attributed to him.

Edward IV, in turn, held Richard in high regard, entrusting him with positions of authority and responsibility within his court. Their relationship was one of mutual respect and affection, with Edward displaying absolute confidence in his younger brother's abilities. Richard, in return, reciprocated this affection with unwavering loyalty and devotion, serving his brother faithfully until the end of his days.

While Richard may have harbored reservations towards the Woodville faction, the family of his brother's queen, he had not harbored any ill will towards his brother's children. On the contrary, he felt some degree of affection for them, as evidenced by his actions following Edward IV's death. Despite the political turmoil that followed, Richard took steps to ensure the safety and well-being of his nephews, even as he ascended to the throne amidst the chaos of civil war.

Richard's coronation was attended by a wide array of nobles and dignitaries, including members of the Woodville faction, who had submitted to his rule. There was simply no party or faction that posed a threat to Richard's reign, rendering any motive for the alleged crime virtually nonexistent.

Furthermore, Richard's treatment of other members of his family, including the daughters of Edward IV and the children of his elder brother Clarence, belies the notion of a man consumed by ambition and ruthlessness. He showed kindness and consideration towards his nieces, offering them protection and support in the tumultuous aftermath of their father's death. Even the young Earl of Warwick, son of

Clarence and a potential rival to Richard's throne, was treated with respect and dignity, being made a member of Richard's household and council.

Rather than viewing them as threats to be eliminated, Richard saw them as family to be cherished and protected.

Chapter Nineteen

When the cardinal questioned the aldermen about their defense of Richard III's actions, they responded with a nuanced perspective. While acknowledging Richard's evil deeds, they pointed to the many good acts undertaken during his reign, often with the consent of Parliament. Indeed, Richard's reign, despite its tarnished legacy, saw moments of progress and stability, underscoring the complexities of political power and the role of governance in shaping history.

Elizabeth Woodville, their mother, played a complex role in the events that followed the prince's disappearance. Initially supporting Henry Tudor in his campaign against Richard III, she later made her peace with Richard and brought her daughters out of sanctuary. Richard's solemn oath, sworn before witnesses, was to protect and provide for her surviving children. This oath, ensured the safety of her daughters.

Two individuals emerged claiming to be Edward and Richard.

The first of these claimants was Lambert Simnel, who initially presented himself as Richard before changing his story and claiming to be Edward Plantagenet, the 17th Earl of Warwick. Simnel's claim gained traction, particularly in Ireland, where he garnered support from various nobles and was crowned as Edward VI. Margaret of York, Duchess of Burgundy and sister of Richard III, formally recognized Simnel as Warwick, adding legitimacy to his claim.

The second claimant, Perkin Warbeck, emerged several years later and asserted that he was indeed Richard, Duke of York, the rightful heir to the throne. Warbeck's claim found support not only in England but also in Scotland, where James IV recognized him as Richard IV.

Richard III had smuggled the princes abroad to the custody of their aunt, the Duchess of Burgundy, where they were raised under false identities. By removing them from sight, Richard sought to prevent them from becoming a focus for opposition, thereby securing his hold on the crown. However, the inability to bring them back to court without once again risking their status as potential threats contributed to the perpetuation of rumors regarding their fate.

About the Author

D.S.Pais

D.S. Pais is an internationally acclaimed, best-selling author known for her vivid imagination and storytelling prowess. From a young age, she was drawn to writing, channeling her creativity primarily into mystery and thriller genres. Her journey into writing began after a stint as an actress in student films and TV series, where she realized her true passion lay in crafting narratives.

When not immersed in the world of words, D.S. Pais finds joy in reading, exploring cinema, indulging in travel adventures, and maintaining her fitness through Pilates and other exercises. She dedicates herself to multiple book projects each year, fueled by her unwavering dedication to the art of storytelling. Her works consistently grace the top ranks of Amazon Best Sellers.

Although born and raised in India, D.S. Pais is now a proud Singaporean Citizen, residing in Singapore with her husband and two children.

YouTube Channel:

https://www.youtube.com/channel/UC3k5wx5eX2_alM0joxJxk5g?sub_confirmation=1

www.ingramcontent.com/pod-product-compliance
Lightning Source LLC
LaVergne TN
LVHW041537070526
838199LV00046B/1715